Susan VanHecke

UNDER THE FREEDOM TREE

Illustrated by London Ladd

⬛ Charlesbridge

Dedicated to the memory of Frank, James, and
Shepard, and all those who bravely determined
their own freedom
　　　—S. V.
To the courageous people of that era and
the descendants who followed
　　　—L. L.

Special thanks to Adam Goodheart, Hodson Trust-Griswold Director at the C. V. Starr Center
for the Study of the American Experience, Washington College, for his expertise and advice.

Published by Charlesbridge, 85 Main Street, Watertown, MA 02472 • (617) 926-0329
www.charlesbridge.com

Library of Congress Cataloging-in-Publication Data
VanHecke, Susan.
    Under the freedom tree / Susan VanHecke; Illustrated by London Ladd.
      p. cm.
    Includes bibliographical references and index.
    ISBN 978-1-58089-550-7 (reinforced for library use)
    ISBN 978-1-60734-634-0 (ebook)
1. Fugitive slaves—Juvenile poetry. 2. Children's poetry, American. I. Ladd, London, illustrator. II. Title.
PS3572.A4387U53 2013
811'.54—dc23   2012038698

Printed in Singapore
(hc) 10 9 8 7 6 5 4 3 2 1

Illustrations done in acrylic, pastel, and colored pencil on primed illustration board
Display type set in Mr Brown, designed by Hipopotam Studio, Poland; text type set in Adobe Goudy
Color separations by KHL Chroma Graphics, Singapore
Printed and bound September 2013 by Imago in Singapore
Production supervision by Brian G. Walker
Designed by Susan Mallory Sherman

1861

May moon
gleams
bright as
Colonel's buttons.

Three slip out unseen.

Frank,
James,
Shepard

scramble down the sandy bank,

hearts drumming,
eyes darting,
knees trembling.

Weathered skiff bobs in rustling rushes.

Quick now, and
quiet!

Stars hold their breath
and so do the three,
four miles from the old oak tree.

Oars dip,
no sound,
silver ripples.

Steal away now,
away.

Away from camp
and Colonel's work,

dragging,
hauling,
digging,
stacking,

until weary bones ache,
torn fingers bleed.

Away
from rifles' crack,
cannons' loud roar.

War.

Away
from Southern soldiers
who would

own them,
work them,
beat them,
sell them,

keep them slaves forever.

Glinting waves
slap rotting wood.
Whispers,
low and shivery.

"What if we're caught?"

Shackles.

The whip.

Sold downriver.

Or worse.

"What will we find
'cross the deep water?"

Better forward than back,
think the three
as they course closer to the old oak tree.

Brass moon fades
and sun climbs high.
Stars and stripes flutter.

General
squints,
spits,
strokes his chin.
Ponders the fate of the three.

Frank,
James,
Shepard.

To his shores they came,
wrapped in night,
to stand bravely before him.

Heads bowed,
hopes bold.

And now comes Colonel's messenger
under white flag of truce.

High on his horse,
here to fetch the three,
two miles from the old oak tree.

"'Tis the rule of the land,
these United States.
You must return our chattel."

Chattel.
Persons as possessions.
Owned and used
like

cows,
pigs,
dogs.

General scowls.
Owl eyes narrow.
People? Or property?
muses he.

Yet wait!

These United States?

"Dear sir," says General,
   smooth as the tide.
"Have you not heard?

"'Twas only yesterday,
   Virginia withdrew.
   Seceded, she did,
   from the union of states.

"So let it be known
   I do here claim and seize
   your 'chattel'
   as enemy property."

Contraband of war
   now are the three,
   as springtime sun
   warms the old oak tree.

Frank,
James,
Shepard.

Three
become forty.

William,
Charlotte,
Waddy.

Then hundreds,
then more.

Runaways.
Stowaways.
Barefoot, mud-crusted.
Better forward than back.

Fortress fills.
Crowded, they spill
beyond the high walls,
beyond the stone gate,

gathering old logs,
scavenging rough planks,
cobbling crude shanties.

Slabtown, they call it.

And still they come,
in patches and tatters.
They come and they come,
a human stream,
thousands upon thousands.

George,
Eliza,
Harry.

Peter,
Sarah,
David.

1862

Now Slabtown fills.
Crowded, they spill
into the ruins
of a city once set aflame.

Torched by Confederates,
Hampton smolders in ash.

There, in Rebels' rubble,

scorched earth,
charred timbers,
burnt brick,

they build and they build.
Grand Contraband Camp.

Days are for Union work,

dragging,
hauling,
digging,
stacking.

Nights, they fall,
spent and hungry,
on cold dirt floors.

But here at Slabtown,
here at the Camp,
they are not
what they once were.

Slabtown is *their* town,
so too the Grand Camp.

A home of their own,
a first for the many.
A home for them all
by the old oak tree.

Missionaries come,
bearing Bibles and news:

"Worship God,
sing praises, and pray.
We shall teach your children."

Reading, writing—
so long forbidden.
But how? But where?
No schoolhouse at Slabtown,
no books at the Camp.

Teacher,
brave teacher,
gathers them all.

As war rages on,
under cool leafy limbs
float boys' and girls' voices:

"A-B-C,
1-2-3,"
sheltered in the shade
of the old oak tree.

1863

New Year's sun
frosts
a pewter-plate sky.

Hundreds huddle under strong, wide branches.

Frank,
James,
Shepard,

and all who came after,

hearts drumming,
eyes darting,
knees trembling.

Boy climbs on crate,
long paper in hand.

Hush now, and
quiet!

Wind holds its breath,
and so does the throng.

With a voice clear, sure, and strong,
boy starts to read:

"'By the President of the United States of America . . .
all persons held as slaves . . .
shall be then,
thenceforward,
and forever
free.'"

Tears rain down
and shouts rise up
to tree's tallest tip,
up, up, to the clouds.

"We're free! We're free!"
Lives changed forever
under the Freedom Tree.

AUTHOR'S NOTE

Under The Freedom Tree is based on events that took place during the Civil War near the Emancipation Oak, a historic southern live oak tree (scientific name: *Quercus virginiana*) that still stands in Hampton, Virginia.

In 1861 in Virginia, many slaves were hired out by their owners to the Confederate forces. They constructed artillery emplacements—fortified dirt mounds to provide cover for weapons and the soldiers firing them—along the southern shore of Hampton Roads harbor. On the northern shore was Fort Monroe, held by the Union army.

The slaves' labor for the Confederates was difficult and exhausting. Even worse, Confederate troops were planning to take the slaves farther south, away from their families, for more war work.

So on the night of May 23, 1861, three slaves—Frank Baker, James Townsend, and Shepard Mallory—escaped the Confederate line and rowed their way across the harbor in a skiff. It was a bold and courageous act. The men were willing to risk brutal, even fatal, punishment for the hope they saw on the other side.

Had the three escaped a few days earlier, they would likely have been returned to their Confederate master, Colonel Charles K. Mallory, as required by the Fugitive Slave Act of 1850. But Virginia had just seceded, declaring itself no longer a part of the United States.

For this reason, General Benjamin Butler, Union commander at Fort Monroe, refused to return the slaves to the colonel. If Virginia was no longer part of the United States, Butler reasoned, then Virginia's citizens were no longer protected by US laws, including the Fugitive Slave Act. Instead, Butler decreed the men "contraband of war," or enemy property.

What did that mean for Baker, Townsend, and Mallory—and the thousands of escaped slaves who flocked to Fort Monroe once word of Butler's decision spread? Certainly, they were not free men, women, and children. At Fort Monroe the contrabands were still treated largely as slaves. Able-bodied men and women were put to work by the Union Army doing the same kinds of labor they had been doing for the Confederates. It wasn't until October 1861 that the Union Army began paying the contrabands for their work.

But "contraband" was surely better than "slave," and seemed a step closer to freedom. By July 1861 more than nine hundred escaped slaves had made their way to Fort Monroe, with more arriving daily. By April 1865 an estimated ten thousand had applied for contraband status. The contrabands constructed their own settlements: the first, Slabtown, just outside the Union base, and the second, Grand Contraband Camp, in the ruins of the city of Hampton. They earned their own money by fishing, oystering, farming, baking, and more.

The Union army was not prepared to provide food, clothing, medical care, and other necessities to the residents of Slabtown and Grand Contraband Camp. When the American Missionary Association (AMA), a Christian group from the North with ties to the abolitionist movement, offered to help, Union leaders quickly agreed. In September 1861 Mary Smith Peake of Hampton, a free black woman working with the AMA, began conducting classes under a massive oak tree two miles from Fort Monroe. It was a brave thing for her to do, as teaching slaves or free blacks to read or write had been illegal in Virginia since 1831. These lessons are considered the first classes at what is now Hampton University, a historically black college.

When Abraham Lincoln signed the Emancipation Proclamation on January 1, 1863, the exciting news spread quickly by telegraph. In Hampton, under the branches of the giant oak where contraband children had learned to read and write, the document was read to the area's black community, most likely on that jubilant New Year's Day, possibly by one of the newly literate contrabands.

Technically, the Emancipation Proclamation freed slaves only in Confederate-held territory. But African Americans across the country rejoiced all the same, viewing the document as a promise of eventual freedom. They were correct. The Thirteenth Amendment to the US Constitution abolished slavery entirely in late 1865.

Today the Emancipation Oak's sprawling branches measure nearly one hundred feet in diameter. It has been designated one of the Ten Great Trees of the World by the National Geographic Society and is part of a National Historic Landmark District at Hampton University. As it has for more than one hundred years, the majestic evergreen remains a living symbol of shelter, perseverance, and hope.

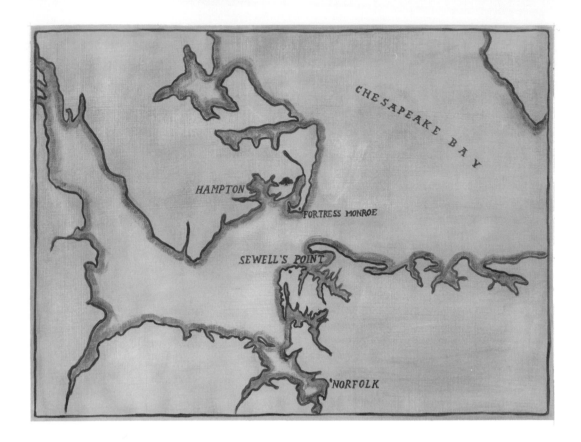

BIBLIOGRAPHY

"Arbor Day Program." *School Journal* 72 (January–June 1906): 248.

Butler, Benjamin F. *Butler's Book: Autobiography and Personal Reminiscences of Major-General Benj. F. Butler.* Boston: A. M. Thayer & Co., 1892.

Casemate Museum, Fort Monroe, VA.

Contraband Historical Society, Hampton, VA. http://www.contrabandhistoricalsociety.org/history.shtml.

Engs, Robert F. *Freedom's First Generation: Black Hampton, Virginia, 1861–1890.* New York: Fordham University Press, 2004.

Goodheart, Adam. *1861: The Civil War Awakening.* New York: Knopf, 2011.

Hampton History Museum. http://www.hampton.gov/history_museum/.

Hampton University. "History." http://www.hamptonu.edu/about/history.cfm.

Hampton University Museum. "University Archives." http://museum.hamptonu.edu/university_archives.cfm.

Lockwood, Rev. Lewis C. *Mary S. Peake, the Colored Teacher at Fortress Monroe.* Boston: American Tract Society, 1862.

Perdue, Charles L., Jr., Thomas E. Barden, and Robert K. Phillips, eds. *Weevils in the Wheat: Interviews with Virginia Ex-Slaves.* Charlottesville: University of Virginia Press, 1976.

Walton-Raji, Angela Y. *My Ancestor's Name* (blog). http://myancestorsname.blogspot.com/.

Wills, Eric. "The Forgotten: The Contraband of America and the Road to Freedom." *Preservation,* May/June 2011, 28–37.